I dedicate this journal to the brave adults that dare to take self-learning into their own hands and become better human beings because of it.

You make the world a better place, and for that I thank you from the bottom of my heart.

praise for jacqueline

JACQUELINE PIRTLE

Who are you?

Your Energetic Truth Awaits

Dear brave adult,

As a holistic practitioner, energetic living expert, and emotional intelligence teacher I have written over 18+ books for adults and children supporting people to live a more conscious, mindful, and happier life.

You can find out more at:
www.freakyhealer.com

Hope you'll take a look!

Happiest,
Jacqueline

claim it!

This journal belongs to:

_____

_____

What's your happy place?
Go there, stay there, and never leave!

Dear brave adult!

It's fact that you understand you are a physical body and most likely know yourself physically pretty well. If not, feel free to slap yourself right at this moment to sense your physicality. Then come back to this!

What I want to clarify though, is: do you also know about the energetics that makes you, *you*?

The energetic value and information of your foundational essence you *came* into this life with, that you have *become* through living your amazing life so far, and will BE in your *future*, is what I am highlighting and inviting you to learn, understand, and use to your advantage by adding THAT to who you already know yourself to be physically.

Only having part of your information, in this case your physical knowledge, makes you vulnerable to everything that is not true for you or is not aligned with who you are because without your energetics, your experience of being alive is solely based on physicality—but, after all, you are a wholesome being made mostly of energy and a little physicality.

Everything is energy at its smallest level. Yours - and everyone else's - job is to sense the energy you are at any given moment and translate the input you receive into thoughts which creates feelings, letting you know how you feel; good or bad. Good feelings signal that you are living according to your true reasons of why you are here as your physical body, whereas bad feelings mean that you are not aligned with yourself fully and completely.

But there is more! Are you ready to figure yourself out energetically and learn everything there is about your energy—starting from when you came into this world, all the way to where you stand today?

This workbook is your tool to accomplish exactly that! It supports you in creating your own Energetic Profile to use as a fountain of wisdom for yourself, and also for everyone you are completing this workbook with.

The Energetic Profile journals come in a series covering all age groups for you to do it alone, with a partner, your family full of kids, or a community—because everyone should learn about their energetics.

Stay open in your heart, mind, ears, and eyes to let this amazing self-discovery do its job, and if needed, take the lead and help others get the most out their workbooks too. Then tap your toes into the art of energetic living by following this guidance and answering the deep questions in this book, helping you to step fully into the truth of who you really are, why you are alive and here, and what this all means to begin with.

So, brave adult, be ready to own your gifts and then maybe, possibly, and hopefully share your wisdom with other people in the world. I know that you have it in you to inspire the whole universe with your newfound insights and can share and spread happiness and fulfillment wherever you go.

Your biggest fan and fellow Energetic Profiler,

Jacqueline

P.S. At the end of this journal you will find some extra pages in case you turn into a writing machine and don't have enough space for all your results and findings—and maybe even your urges to doodle or draw. I hope you go fill them up and have a blast!

DAY 1

Doubt — we all experience it. Who, what, where, when has it surfaced for you?

Close your eyes, take a deep breath, then pinch yourself as hard or soft as you want and wherever you feel most comfortable—make sure you feel this important self-squeeze consciously.

How did this awakening pinch feel on your skin? How did it feel inside of you? What thoughts surfaced with this pinch? If needed, give yourself another pinch then note down the revelations of your inner and outer findings:

_____

_____

_____

Now that you have proof of your physical existence, become aware that you also have the needed evidence of you being energy since feelings, thoughts, inner-inputs, and even pains are energies—hence, they are not tangible.

That means any doubt you might have about your energetic existence is not real. You and doubt can part ways, setting you free to fully open yourself up to the energetic inner work you have committed yourself to here.

How do you feel, so free, with so much possibility to learn about your energetic meaning? Make your newfound feeling list below, for you to come back to whenever you need a refresher:

_____

_____

_____

_____

_____

DAY 2

Even your name is energy!

Write your full name(s) on the line below:

_____

What's your favorite way to say your name(s)? How do you like your name(s) pronounced? Test how they sound by mumbling them, saying them softly or loudly, or even yell them from the top of your lungs. How does it feel, being so actively involved with your name(s)? What clarity do you receive by expressing your name(s) so firmly?

_____
_____
_____
_____

Next, how do you feel about your name(s)? What information and meaning does it, or do they, hold for you? What's special about your name(s)? Are they representing a certain energy, strength, power, talent, or even a specific color? Write down the insights into the energies of your name(s).

_____
_____
_____
_____
_____
_____
_____
_____
_____

Who Are You?

DAY 3

Time to get your numbers straight!

Smile and write down your full birth date:

_____

Then take your birth day number and stare only at that numeral. Don't worry, we're not playing favorites here, your other birth numbers will get your full attention over the next few days.

What does focusing on your unique birth day make you feel? Do you feel an uplift in emotions, a heaviness, lightness, or something else? Is there a flair of something special attached to that number; luck, wisdom, gift, or something else? What does this number represent to you?

Go on, journal about the energies, insights, feelings, thoughts, that your brilliant birth day number holds.

_____
_____
_____
_____
_____
_____
_____
_____
_____
_____
_____
_____
_____
_____

Mirror mirror on the wall, what's the most amazing month of all?

It's time to brag a little by writing your special birth month below:

_____

Now look at your unique birth month, see it for the brilliant number (or word) it is.

Close your eyes, take some deep breaths until relaxation takes over to the point where you almost fall asleep. There, in that right-before-snoozing energy, visualize your fabulous birth month. Think of it, feel it, and see it!

Still with closed eyes, ask to have a meeting with your birth month, in which you discuss the deep meaning and energetic value to discover how your month feels to you; for instance does it seem humongous or tiny, like a force or a gentle drift, strong or intelligent, fun or strict?

Once the meeting is over and you got what you need, open your eyes and jot down all that you saw, felt, thought, and now know.

_____
_____
_____
_____
_____
_____
_____
_____
_____
_____
_____
_____

Not all that's bigger is better—or is it?

Go ahead and write down your big birth year number, then love it like you mean it by outstaring this numeral with your biggest admiration.

_____

Next breathe, smile, and close your eyes! Then take on the challenge to ask yourself, and your birth year, some big questions:

What's the significance of my birth year to me? What energy do I sense thinking of this big number? Is there a certain power that comes with this year, one I feel when looking at it?

What is my birth year telling me about its value and energy?

Trust all insights you receive, and try not to let yourself get psyched out if things don't make sense. Can you do that?

Start writing down your compelling new knowledge:

_____
_____
_____
_____
_____
_____
_____
_____
_____
_____
_____
_____

DAY 6

Party like a kid!

Pretend today is your birthday, and shush any inner chatter that says differently. Just party on!

What insanely mouthwatering cake will you want—what flavor, shape, color, and decoration will you choose? Make it big, gorgeous, delicious, and just the way you like. Best of all, it's all yours, so why hold back since it's imaginary and you won't have to work it off; yet still gain the energetic value of bliss?

Now, every birthday cake is crowned by candles and yours is no different. How many candles are there, or more appropriately, how old are you today, for real? Have no mercy and write your fabulous age on the line:

_____

Get comfy with your age by lovingly looking at it with a smile - you are still young - then squeeze out all the knowledge you can get:

How do you feel being this young? What energy does your age carry for you? What are the emotions behind your fabulous age? What does it all mean to you, being your age?

And since being silly never hurts, ask your age how it would dress to impress, if it could.

_____
_____
_____
_____
_____
_____

DAY 7

What time is it?

It's *your* time! Write down your unique hour and minute of your glorious arrival on earth. Then time-spiral back to the moment of your birth, stop the clock, and BE there in stillness for a bit.

_____

Once all you can see and feel is your birth hour, ask yourself about the quality of energy that was present at your "hello world" event? Take it even further, sense into the meaning this hour (the numeral itself) has for you? What are the insights of the hour you started being you?

_____
_____
_____
_____
_____
_____
_____

Next comes your minute. Look at this magical number; what does your minute-timing feel like? What is the energy of your unique minute?

_____
_____
_____
_____
_____
_____
_____

DAY 8

YOU are such a baby!

Big reveal: once upon a time, you were the size of a little pea and the place at which you were born is what's in the spotlight today. Write down the name of your birthplace:

_____

What is your first immediate impression when reading and looking at the name of your birthplace?

_____

_____

Nothing is ever a coincidence, but always meant to be. This also counts for your sacred birthplace, where you took your first breath and saw the initial glimmer of earth. Your birthplace is meant to be yours, and holds immense truth about who you really are.

So close your eyes, visualize how it looked *where* and *when* you were born. Feel into the energy that was present. Let it all sink in; every feeling, thought, noise, smell, and insight.

Then, journal about your instinctual wisdom and the energy your unique birth place holds: not just what it means to you, but also the energy you were blessed with from the start.

_____

_____

_____

_____

_____

_____

DAY 9

Energy here, there, and everywhere!

It's proven by science that everything at its smallest particle is energy, making energy all there is. You are made of energy, and everything about life is always about energy. Everything you do, say, think, and feel is energy and when you breathe or walk you are actively energy. Energy is always new, moving, and changing because that's how energy behaves. So think of yourself as a walking cloud of energy, constantly moving and changing in a life that's also energy.

To familiarize yourself with this fact ask yourself: How big is my energy right now? How does my energy feel, what information does my energetic state carry? You can also ask your energy for answers by closing your eyes and taking a deep breath, establishing a potent connection. Then create a baseline by rating your energy from 1 - 10 (1 being lowest, 10 being highest).

_____

_____

Next, close your eyes and time travel to the moment you took your first breath—then take that first breath of yours! Make it deep and powerful. What energy does your first puff have—do you see sparks or fireworks? Do you sense the extreme force and power this first clear "Yes!" to life represents? Describe the **life-force energy** you came into this world with and know that this strong **energy** is yours to BE and live your whole life.

_____
_____
_____
_____
_____

Knock, knock. Who's there?

No, you're not whacky just because of the inner voice in your head, heart, stomach, or literally anywhere. On the contrary, this inner chitter-chatter is your energetic intelligence, one you want to push further all the way into being your super-talent. So where do you normally hear, feel, or sense your inner vocalization?

_____

_____

_____

It's of utmost value to be aware of your inner voice, also known as intuition or instinct, but it's even more important to listen to it and accept what it says by following the guidance you receive with the utmost trust. Your inner voice has your back and is always right, so don't even think of arguing it away, and it's unique to you—it's energy, your energy.

Today you'll practice hearing the loudest one of all, your head voice. So close your eyes, take a deep breath and focus on hearing how it sounds and what it says.

Is it a whisper, or more like a trombone? What is it saying? Ask your head voice: "Do you hear me?" "What do you want to tell me?" "What do I need to know about myself?"

Journal about it, and promise yourself to hear it from now on.

_____

_____

_____

_____

_____

_____

Your heart knows you, and to strengthen your trust in it, rehearse the following mantra often:

"My heart knows best and always points me towards who I am, what I want, and what's right for me. It's where I feel my love, happiness, satisfaction, and all other good-feeling emotions."

How does saying these words make you feel? Describe it in detail:

_____

_____

Next up; how big is the love in your heart? How capable are you of experiencing pure love, bliss, and happiness—how can you better yourself in that? Take what you write as a great heart-love baseline and reality check!

_____

_____

_____

Now put your hands on your heart, feel it beating. Take a deep breath. Can you hear your heart's voice, feel its energy? Listen! What is telling you? Ask: "What and how do I feel?"

Time for the best love story ever, the tale of you and your heart!

_____

_____

_____

_____

_____

_____

_____

A cave so dark!

Your stomach! It's cave-y, dark, warm, and outfitted with one of your most powerful walkie-talkie functions—your gut instinct, a deep clear knowing constantly delivering messages for you to recognize.

Your gut voice feels like you know that you just *know*, you can't explain why or where it's coming from you truly just *know*—and probably also just wish everyone else would accept your knowing. Because you know that you *know*!

How do you feel when you just know—what is the energetic value of you knowing?

_____

_____

_____

_____

Let's practice, so you can hear your gut instinct even clearer! Close your eyes, put your hands on your stomach, and take a deep breath. Then ask away… "What do I know, what am I certain of?" "What do I need to know?" "What do I want to know?"

Trust what you *know* and write it all down:

_____

_____

_____

_____

_____

_____

_____

You got them, so use them!

Many times your lungs are underused (habitual shallow breathing) or left to fend for themselves in autopilot because hey, they know what to do and will do what they must do.

But what if you would fill your oxygen tanks while focusing on them? You would feel how every inhale has the power of expanding you in ways that lets infinite amounts of life-energy enter your system, while every exhale cleanses you by letting out whatever is not serving you.

Go on, take a truly focused breath right now. How does it feel, filling up with such worth?

_____

_____

Next, let's go back to your first breath again, just like you did on Day 9. Close your eyes, imagine being born right now, then take your first breath as that baby you.

How does your first breath even feel? Is there a sprinkle of strength, determination, expectation, or force in it? Journal brave one, this one is a big detail to remember!

_____

_____

_____

_____

_____

Every breath now has that same value like your first breath, meaning you can feel that amazing at all times because you ARE this amazing energy every time you breath in and out.

DAY 14

Focus baby, focus!

Why? Because your whys hold not only your deepest secrets, blockages, hold-backs and more, but also your purest wishes, dreams, what you are really made of and here to do.

Today that's where you will point your clarity antennas, so get ready to go all clear with your little and big whys, to catch knowledge and understanding, receive answers, and be in awe of findings you didn't even know existed.

Take a deep breath, close your beautiful eyes, then ask these potent questions: "What am I here to do on earth?" "What energy am I here to BE and share?" "What is my job, besides being alive, living as a human being, and journaling through this shifting workbook?" "What are my whys?"

You get to talk about you, so get to it!

_____
_____
_____
_____
_____
_____
_____
_____
_____
_____
_____
_____
_____
_____
_____

Passion-Blind.

Are you or are you not aware of all your passions? Being unaware of what gets your heart singing and creativity fired up is a no-go zone if you want to live an energetically aligned life.

Go deep and search for what you are passionate about! Choose the ones that if you can't have them or do them you'll throw an adult fit—let's not forget what you will do if someone stands between you and your passions, or all that you will do to get what you love so much.

To clarify: Real aligned passions create harmony, inner peace, and deep satisfaction in and for you when following them, while turning a blind eye to them is unleashing havoc in your life.

Be notified: unaligned - not coming from your heart - passions create unrest when chasing them.

So, what would you give anything for, because without it your life seems literally over? What would you trade favorites for in order to do or have? How does your most passionate you show up? What energy are you charged with when deeply passionate—and determine the opposite, how do you feel when passion has left your side?

_____
_____
_____
_____
_____
_____
_____
_____
_____

Materialism turned good!

Pick three material things that you love, love, love and note down the purpose they serve for you, what makes them so loved:

1._____

2._____

3._____

Next, write about your own purpose in life, besides being alive and fulfilling whatever role you are living at the moment.

What is your strongest and most important purpose? Come up with many more. What energies do your purposes carry? How are you using your purposes, who are you helping with your purposes? What are the meanings of your purposes and how do they make you feel?

Purposefully journal about this important part of you.

_____
_____
_____
_____
_____
_____
_____
_____
_____
_____
_____
_____

Time to show off!

Think of 2 people you admire for their talented ways of living their lives. List them below. Why do you see them as superstars? What impresses you about them, what is it they have that inspires you? Note down your thoughts:

_____

_____

_____

_____

Your turn! Stand in front of the mirror, point the finger at yourself, and think about what impresses you about yourself. Not an easy task, but you have the talent to get to your own admiration-truth. Beware, once you start you'll be on a roll and not able to stop. That's when you have hit the jackpot because you have dug up your superpower called self-worth, a talent you already possess.

Another option is to opt for an out-of-body experience by stepping outside yourself and looking through the eyes of others; what do they see in you?

List at least 5 of your fabulous gifts! How do they make you feel? What are you doing with them?

_____

_____

_____

_____

_____

_____

_____

_____

To love or not to love? Is that even a question since love is the solution to everything?

There are many different varieties of love. Yes, some are really hurtful or seem like they don't fix anything, but fact is love uplifts everything—just think about when love was the most magnificent state you have ever been in, or the miracles that happen through the energy of love, and let's not forget the loving ways of gratitude, happiness, joy, and bliss.

Depending on who or what you are loving, the energy of love differs in experience—the love for loved ones is unlike the love for things, activities, adventures, fun times, or for being lazy, sleeping, and napping. And yet, it's all love!

But the most powerful love that you really have to know inside and out is one that no one else but you can feel; your self love. It's also the only love that can always solve everything for you.

How does your love for yourself feel? How do you practice it, and what's a good measurement for how much you love yourself?

_____

_____

Scan your whole body by closing your eyes and sensing where your love is present. Start at your heart since that is love's birthplace and a great baseline for how love feels for you, then scan up and down while writing about your sensations.

_____

_____

_____

_____

DAY 19

Sweet for the win! What's your favorite sweet treat?

_____

Can you get your hands on it right now? If not, what treat do you have available? Then armed with sweets, which can cancel out any sourness, get ready to dig into your emotions without the faintest wish to escape. Starting with the feelings you love, what are some of your strongest emotions? How do you feel, think, talk, act, look when they arise?

_____

_____

_____

_____

_____

Next, give your strongest emotions you don't like, or have trouble getting control of, the stage. What are they and how do they feel when in action? What are some possible changes you can make to shift yourself into a better state when they arrive? Make sure your plan entails embracing all your feelings, growing self-pride for being able to feel that strongly, and wanting to react in ways that are better for you.

_____

_____

_____

_____

_____

_____

_____

_____

Noggin' much to talk about!

Your brain is a willing asset, ready for you to take advantage of. Question is, are you?

How much do you like your brain and how do you feel about your thinking machine? Are you using your noggin' and smartness to the full extent, or are you quite often showing up without representing how genius you are—playing way too small? If yes, when are these moments, what is the trigger, where do they take place, and who's involved?

_____

_____

Let's take a trip! Imagine traveling into your brain to do a little investigative research. Ready, set, zip, and you're in!

How does it look in your brainy world, how is it being in there? What vibes are present, what energies is your brain filled with? Look around, what is the condition of your brain; is it nourished, positive, alive and thriving?

Then take an imaginary moment to sit down in there and listen to what your brain is telling you.

Quick, use that brain power and note down your smart findings!

_____

_____

_____

_____

_____

_____

_____

DAY 21

Your tornado of thoughts? Not just your imagination!

You have thousands of thoughts every single day giving you thousand of possibilities to be aligned or unaligned, because thoughts create feelings and depending on their quality - positive or negative - they determine if you feel good (aligned) or not (unaligned.) The real kicker is that the factory of your thoughts, your strong mind, runs on your old beliefs, programs, and habits which most often don't serve you in thinking and feeling the best that you could. Your mind also loves being in charge and takes over when you're on autopilot; not focused in your now or thinking about the past or future. The solution to feel better is twofold:

1. Stay in your *now*, putting you in charge of acknowledging the quality of your thoughts right when they happen.

2. Reprogram your thoughts by shifting to better feeling ones right on the spot.

Thinking positively feeds your mind positive energy, elevating you into a high-for-life frequency. What are your favorite positive thoughts and how do you feel when thinking them?

_____

_____

_____

What about the negative ones, how do you feel thinking them?

_____

_____

_____

_____

_____

DAY 22

Reaching for the stars!

When was the last time you truly focused on your wishes and dreams and not just on what needs to get done, what's lacking, or what you are supposed to be? Note down when:

_____

Wishing, desiring, yearning or longing is not just a modern luxury-practice or something silly to do. It's a direct line to who you really are, because what you are wishing for is unique to you and how you feel. What you want is a huge part of you!

So dive deep into the delicious frequency of wishing by asking yourself: "What are my truest wishes and dreams—what excites me the most, what gives me fuel and vividness, what makes me feel alive, and what accomplishments lift me up?" "What limitless and heartfelt wishes and dreams do I have?"

Go on, it's wishlist time! Make it brilliant, feel your excitement and I-can't-wait energy while writing every line, and end them with expectant gratitude by saying: "Thank you, I can't wait!" Then off you go, energized and fulfilled with a spark in your eyes.

_____
_____
_____
_____
_____
_____
_____
_____
_____

Who Are You?

DAY 23

You deserve to be happy!

But in order to know what happy means to you, investigation is needed. So, what's your happy place? What energy is happiness? How does your personal happy life look and feel like? What brings you joy and gets you into a satisfied state, where you can't stop singing, dancing, and playing? What's adventurous, healthy, abundant, successful, and crazy to you? What are your greatest memories from the past and what are your coolest visions for your future? Who's involved, and what's the bliss all about?

Write your happy story, make it aligned and feel-good:

_____

_____

_____

_____

_____

_____

_____

_____

_____

_____

_____

_____

_____

_____

_____

_____

_____

_____

Are you a foodie?

Food is not just food. It's nutrition, and when consciously devoured, has impactful healing for you—plus it differs for everyone uniquely. But food also has a complicated trouble-energy attached for many; we won't go into the why of that here. Instead let's focus on you finding your food truths, eliminating the quest of understanding these troubles.

Ask yourself: "What is food for me, what meaning does it have?" "How do I feel when I eat?" "What do I enjoy about food and what energetic value does this enjoyment have?" "What ways do I love to eat most: fast, slow, small amounts or large plates, sitting down or walking around, out in nature or inside, at home or in a restaurant, at a table, on the sofa, in bed?" "With whom do I enjoy meals most; alone, with others, in small or large groups?" "Do the smacking noises get to me?"

Also, what energies do your favorite yummies have and fill you with? What energies do your least liked foods have, and why?

Food is also art, creative, and fun; how can you make your food-times a more high-for-life energy?

_____

_____

_____

_____

_____

_____

_____

_____

_____

_____

The winner wins!

Fact is everyone can be a winner, because every winner once started as a beginner.

So take a deep breath and close your eyes, keep breathing deeply and feel how much life you are filling yourself with, how much space you are creating for yourself, and how this amazing oxygen holds more energy you thought is possible. Then, imagine a winning movie that goes something like this:

You are a winner, having a winner day, winning at whatever you are doing. You are a winner!

Step into this winner clip as the main actor, since it's all about you: you are the winner, winning at everything. Feel your stardom in this!

When ready, note down your answers to the following:

How do you feel, what is your energy, being a winner? What are you doing, what is the winning experience you are having—what is winning for you? Are you smiling? What are you wearing? Do you feel powerful and happy? Who is in the winner movie with you, what do the surroundings look like, where does your winner experience take place?

_____

_____

_____

_____

_____

_____

_____

_____

_____

DAY 26

Congratulations, look at all the extra self-knowledge you gained! Bravo! Time to do some fact checking.

Fact 1:

What should the world know about you? What do you want your family, loved ones, friends, co-workers, and people you encounter every day to know about you? What are you proud of yourself for?

_____

_____

_____

_____

_____

_____

_____

_____

_____

_____

_____

_____

_____

_____

_____

_____

_____

_____

_____

_____

_____

Fact 2:

Imagine you can do whatever you want to do—even if you are already practicing such a grand lifestyle. What more, or different, do you want it to be? How do you want to do it? Where will you do your favorite thing, and what will you need so you can do what you want to do?

_____

_____

_____

_____

_____

_____

_____

_____

_____

_____

_____

_____

_____

_____

_____

_____

_____

_____

_____

_____

Fact 3:

You have a given intellect; emotionally, thoughtfully, mindfully, physically, spiritually, energetically, and more! Your genius is always right there for you and with you, because it is YOU! List all your intellects you can think of! How are you using them? How do they make you feel? How can your smarts help others?

_____

_____

_____

_____

_____

_____

_____

_____

_____

_____

_____

_____

_____

_____

_____

_____

_____

_____

_____

_____

_____

_____

_____

DAY 29

Fact 4:

Imagine you could choose your perfect life. How would you like your life to be? Where would you want to live? What does it look like there?

_____

_____

_____

_____

_____

_____

_____

_____

_____

_____

_____

_____

_____

_____

_____

_____

_____

_____

_____

_____

_____

_____

_____

Fact 5:

Imagine you get to give one gift (or more) to the world, to make it kinder, safer, more peaceful. What would that be?

_____
_____
_____
_____
_____
_____
_____
_____
_____
_____
_____
_____
_____
_____
_____
_____
_____
_____
_____
_____
_____
_____
_____
_____

bonus

Because hey, nobody wants the good stuff to end.

So keep on profiling, there's still so much to find out about yourself!

DAY 31

Find 15 words that describe you perfectly. How do these descriptions make you feel and what can you do better to live that truer you?

_____

_____

_____

_____

_____

_____

_____

_____

_____

_____

_____

_____

_____

_____

_____

_____

_____

_____

_____

_____

_____

_____

_____

_____

_____

DAY 32

List 15 foods that you love. How do you feel eating them? Can you swap the unhealthy ones for healthier options? What are those better options? How about happier ways to eat, can you make changes there too?

_____
_____
_____
_____
_____
_____
_____
_____
_____
_____
_____
_____
_____
_____
_____
_____
_____
_____
_____
_____
_____
_____
_____
_____

Name 15 activities, adventures, and things you want to do just because they make you happy:

_____

_____

_____

_____

_____

_____

_____

_____

_____

_____

_____

_____

_____

_____

_____

_____

_____

_____

_____

_____

_____

_____

_____

_____

_____

_____

_____

Come up with 15 mantras that shift you into the high energy of kindness, feeling compassion for yourself and for others. Say, think, and feel them often in your days.

Examples:

I AM an enjoyer of random acts of kindness.

Kindness fills every single cell of my being with healing, abundance, and happiness.

_____

_____

_____

_____

_____

_____

_____

_____

_____

_____

_____

_____

_____

_____

_____

_____

_____

_____

_____

_____

What makes the world a better place? How can you contribute to these solutions? List at least 15 of these ideas:

_____
_____
_____
_____
_____
_____
_____
_____
_____
_____
_____
_____
_____
_____
_____
_____
_____
_____
_____
_____
_____
_____
_____
_____
_____
_____
_____
_____
_____
_____

extra pages

How cool is it that you don't have to sweat the small stuff—like not having enough space for all your results and findings or to refrain from doodling or drawing too?

Just come on over here and use these extra pages for whatever needs you have to scratch, and most importantly, have a blast while you're at it.

Who Are You?

Who Are You?

thank you!

Let's be honest here… I have a dream team!

I could not have finished this book without the help of talented, creative, and phenomenal professionals and the guidance of ALL children in my life.

From the bottom of my heart, I want to thank Zoe Pirtle for her editorial mastery; kingwoodcreations.com for their fun and polished book cover design; and madiouART.com for an amazing photo shoot.

I'd also like to extend a huge "Thank You!" to all fans of my work and books—I created this beautiful journal for ALL adults in this universe.

Life is spectacular with you on my side!

and last but not least

I truly hope you enjoyed this journal as much as I loved writing it, and if that's so, it would be wonderful if you could take a short minute and leave a review at freakyhealer.com, on Amazon.com, and Goodreads.com as soon as you can.

Your kind feedback helps other adults find my books more easily, and be happy faster. Consider it a happy deed for the people of the world. Thank you!

To find out more about my work and books check out:

www.freakyhealer.com

Jacqueline's Amazon Author Page

about the author

Jacqueline Pirtle is an internationally-renowned Mindful Happiness expert and the bestselling author of over 18+ transformational personal growth books for adults and children.

She is a thought leader in the fields of mindfulness, happiness, energy work, energetic living and businessing, wholesome healing, and the teachings of one's soul.

Jacqueline has over 28 years of experience and has helped thousands of clients all over the world to discover their own happiness and how to live a conscious and mindfully aligned life filled with health, happiness, abundance, and success.

As the owner of *FreakyHealer* she has shared her solid teachings through her bestselling books, podcasts *The Weekly Freak & The Corporate Happiness Show*, sessions, workshops, courses and programs, talks and presentations with clients worldwide. She holds international degrees in holistic health and natural living and is certified in hypnosis for PTSD and a Reiki Master.

Her highly effective healing work has been featured in print and online magazines, podcasts, radio shows, on TV, and in the documentaries *The Overly Emotional Child* by *Learning Success*, available on *Amazon Prime* and Hacking Happiness.